EXCURSION to Loweswater

EXCURSION to *Loweswater*

A LAKELAND VISIT 1865

Mary Hodgson and Lydia Lunt

Introduction by Christopher Newsom

Macdonald Orbis

A *Macdonald Orbis* BOOK

Text and illustration copyright © 1987 Adam Hodgkin

Introduction copyright © 1987 Christopher Newsom

First published in Great Britain in 1987
by Macdonald & Co (Publishers) Ltd
London & Sydney

A member of BPCC plc

British Library Cataloguing in Publication Data

Hodgson, Mary
Excursion to Loweswater
1. Lake District (England) — Description
and travel
I. Title II. Lunt, L.M. III. Newsom,
Christopher
914.27'80483   DA670.L1
ISBN 0-356-14541-7

Excursion to Loweswater was conceived, edited and designed
by Thames Head, a division of BLA Publishing Limited
Blakes
Much Hadham
Hertfordshire SG10 6BT
United Kingdom

Publisher
Martin Marix Evans

Design and Production
David Playne

Editor
Gill Davies

Designers
Heather Church Dave Ganderton Marc Langley

Typeset in Century Schoolbook by Playne Books and
processed by Townsend Typesetter Limited, Worcester

Printed and bound in Italy by
New Interlitho

Reproduction by F.E. Burman, London

Macdonald & Co (Publishers) Ltd
Greater London House
Hampstead Road
London NW1 7QX

Acknowledgements

*Although there are many books about the Lake District
published every year, there are only two writers who, in
my opinion, deserve to be read and read again — Norman
Nicholson and Molly Lefebure. My indebtedness to
them is heartfelt.*

*There is an indebtedness of another kind to Gwen
Mathews, Bookseller in Carlisle, and to Dorothy and
Colin Allen of Askham.*

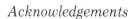

Contents

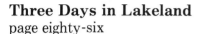

Three Days in Lakeland
page eighty-six

Commentary on the illustrations
page one hundred and forty-one

Up the steep rugged pathway of Borrowdale Haws,
'Twas truly a clamber of wonderful sort;
For the drizzle of mist scarcely troubled our sport,
Though of thorough protection we really were
                    shorn,
        And 'twas wonder we bore it so well.

But the bold front of Honister, lofty and steep,
Where high overhead the cool vapours did creep,
        Stood out in his grandeur at length,
Below him we drove in a perilous way
To where down in the valley dark Buttermere lay,
And where Crummock's deep waters acknowledge
                    the sway
        Of Grasemoor's immovable strength.

eight

Introduction

by Christopher Newsom

The original album of *Excursion to Loweswater* is a
delightful thank-you present, given to Robert and Rachel
Jackson of Waterend in Cumberland by their weekend
guests from Manchester. Bound in gold-tooled leather, the
journal is handwritten and illustrated both in pen-and-ink
and in watercolours, mainly by Mary Hodgson who also
wrote the poem. The book was preserved and passed down
through generations of Quaker families, and came to the
present owner through his great-aunt, Lucy Violet
Holdsworth. Unfortunately, nothing is known of the
authors, the members of the party or their hosts, other than
what can be deduced from the journal itself.

The journey took place in July 1865, and "forty-four
numbered the party; seventeen ladies, twenty-seven
gentlemen". There was certainly an element of pilgrimage in
the Excursion. Both hosts and visitors were Quakers,
members of the Society of Friends founded by George Fox
over two hundred years earlier. Fox's base of operations was
Swarthmore Hall near Ulverston, some thirty miles to the
south of Loweswater, and his journals have many
references to his visits to Cockermouth, Derwent Water,
Kendal and other Lake District towns.

Quakerism was the most successful of the 17th-century
attempts to escape the oppressiveness of the established
church on the one hand and the straightjacket of Calvinism

on the other, and to recover the simplicities of 1st-century Christianity. Hence the Quakers' attempt to abandon the 'pagan' names of months and days. 'First Day Schools' were therefore the Quaker version of Sunday schools. These started in Birmingham in 1840; they came later than and were different from what we think of today as Sunday schools, being devoted to adult education.

Excursion to Loweswater suggests that the Manchester First-Day School was far from solemn. The teachers' energy, cheerfulness and especially their eagerness to perceive the hand of their Maker in the beauty of the Lake District are evident in this journal, as well as their wish to visit the scenes of Fox's ministry. But essentially it seems they were just tourists — like so many of us today, seeking simply to enjoy themselves.

That the visitors were influenced in their enthusiasm by their literary and artistic heritage is indicated in the account of the journey and shown markedly in the selection of subjects for illustration. A brief outline of that heritage may help when retracing the Excursion today.

Tourism in general, and that of the Lake District in particular, is a relatively modern amusement. It is often supposed that such visits to the Lake District were, if not invented by, at least first inspired by William Wordsworth. In fact Wordsworth did not really become popular until about 1830. His guide book, however, once it was no longer associated with Wilkinson's book of engravings, for which it had been written as an introduction in 1810, was reprinted many times.

The closure of the Continent during the troubles of 1789 to 1815 gave a tremendous boost to Lakeland tourism; this was paralleled by a shift in aesthetic appreciation as the Romantic began to mingle with the Picturesque. The artists had begun to arrive. Among them was J.W.M. Turner who had executed two plates for Samuel Rogers' *Poems* published in 1834. Other less-remembered artists toured, with engravings in mind, from the late 18th century, but with the invention of steel engraving the market for, and

Askham Church by William Green. "How sacred the spirit by which our forefathers were directed! The religio loci *is no where violated by these unstinted yet unpretending works of human hands." Askham lies outside the central Lakes, but this engraving gives a view of the vernacular architecture.*

distribution of, 'views' became almost limitless. A tourist industry began.

The first 'literary' travellers in the Lake District (and travellers they were — not tourists) were Celia Fiennes and Daniel Defoe. Charles Avison, a Newcastle musician was inspired by a visit to Derwent Water to declaim "here is beauty indeed — Beauty lying in the lap of Hourrour". These words were echoed by the prominent national poet Thomas Gray in 1775:

"Behind you are the magnificent heights of Walla-crag; opposite lie the thick hanging woods of Lord Egremont, and Newland-valley with green and smiling fields embosm'd in the dark cliffs; to the left the jaws of Borodale, with that turbulent Chaos of mountain behind mountain roll'd in confusion; beneath you, and stretching far away to the right, the shining purity of the Lake, just ruffled by the breeze enough to shew it is alive, reflecting rocks, woods, fields, and inverted tops of mountains, with the white buildings of Keswick, Crosthwait-church, and Skiddaw for a back-ground at distance."

It is alleged that Gray closed the curtains of his carriage when passing through the Jaws of Borrowdale!

At some time, and I suspect that here Wordsworth had some influence, it began to be felt that a visit to the Lakes was somehow 'improving'.

Earlier in the century, the educated were made aware of a group of poets who had been dubbed, or rather snubbed, by the editor of the influential *Edinburgh Review* as "Lake

Poets". This group was headed by William Wordsworth and included Samuel Taylor Coleridge, Robert Southey, and others less known today, such as John Wilson ('Christopher North'), Charles Lloyd (whose family bank survives) and other minor poets. Thomas de Quincey, though not a poet, was a successful, and often scurrilous, essayist. He took over Dove Cottage after the Wordsworths, but then went away to Edinburgh leaving the cottage as a book store.

Coleridge was not really a Lake Poet at all. Most of his poetry was written elsewhere and he spent most of his time in the south of England or abroad. His wife and children were sheltered by Southey for many years at Greta Hall in Keswick. Coleridge's journal *The Friend*, in its first edition, was written in Grasmere and printed in Penrith. He was, however, the first Lakeland rock climber, and he wrote a vivid description of a descent of Broad Stand on Scafell.

Robert Southey, Poet Laureate, was prolific in prose and verse, and this expenditure of effort eventually drove him out of his mind. He is mainly remembered for three things: a poem on the Falls of Lodore, the story of Goldilocks and the Three Bears, and a rather good recipe for gooseberry pie.

The arrival of the railways, industrial arteries, led to the construction of the branch line to Windermere, which was bitterly opposed by Wordsworth (though privately he bought shares) but welcomed by others who thought that some form of civilization might easily and usefully be brought to the unenlightened inhabitants.

As a result of improved access (echoed a century later with the construction of the M6 motorway), tourist facilities

Viaduct on the Kendal and Windermere Railway in 1847.
A print published the year the railway was opened.

grew. Bowness-on-Windermere, in particular, expanded, and around Windermere Manchester industrialists were able to build mansions on the shores of the lake. The railway also made possible the mini-weekend and even the day trip to Bowness or Keswick.

fourteen

The weather takes precedence in any discussion of the Lakes. July and August, which for school teachers in every age are The Holidays are almost the two wettest months of the year. The effects of this on our party we shall see. The idea of the rain "coming down like stair-rods" is graphically portrayed. Happily it cleared, as it always does.

Finally, to set the scene, it may be useful to remember what events were taking place beyond the boundaries of the Lake District: The American Civil War had come to an end. President Lincoln lay dead at the hand of an assassin. The Lancashire Cotton Famine was over. There was a cholera outbreak in 1865 but Manchester had not yet appointed a Medical Officer of Health. The Great Eastern was laying the second, and successful, trans-Atlantic cable. Convicts were still being transported to western Australia, and New Zealand was embroiled in Maori wars. Nearer home, the Russians were busy annexing Tashkent.

Meanwhile, the world of the Arts presented an interesting backcloth to these events. A potent reminder of contemporary taste is the creation of the Albert Memorial — by extraordinary contrast, Whistler was at the same time exhibiting 'The Little White Girl'. Thackeray had just died, George Eliot was busy writing and Charles Dickens had just published *Our Mutual Friend.* Charles Kingsley's *The Water Babies* had recently arrived on the bookselves, and Wilkie Collins was enjoying great success with *The Woman in White.*

* * * * * * *

Today, if you stand with your back to the telephone box at Loweswater, the view remains unchanged, or so we would like to think; the artificial regeneration of woodland and the activities of sympathetic conservationists have no doubt had their effect. I am not sure that Ambleside has much changed; I have doubts about Keswick; the Honister has been transformed.

To begin at the beginning; the forty-four tourists arrived at the newly opened railway station at Windermere (now a supermarket) in the pouring rain. They had left Manchester in two parties, one on Friday evening, the other at 2 am on Saturday, to arrive in time for breakfast. The first objective was Ambleside to see a waterfall, and to see it before breakfast. The Victorians seem to have been fascinated by waterfalls. One wonders why? Symptomatic, I suppose, is the disappearance of Holmes and Moriarty over the Reichenbach Falls. The Lakeland waterfalls are in any case disappointing except after heavy rain. Many had special approach steps constructed and wooden bridges for viewing, now much decayed.

The tourists' way led them towards Rydal and Grasmere, in "five wagonettes, each with two horses, and a one-horse phaëton". On their left, at The Knoll, lived the philanthropist Harriet Martineau. This prestigious lady played a part in the Abolition of Slavery, as well as writing many educational tracts and guides to the Lakes. She was visited by Charlotte Brontë, George Eliot, and Emerson who spent two days here. Further along, on the right, they passed Rydal Mount, Wordsworth's last home (which I think is a more evocative place to visit than Dove Cottage).

Ambleside, Westmorland. Mary Hodgson's drawing of their "snug quarters" has been done with this in front of her.

The way from here to Grasmere is interesting. Nab Cottage, now slightly by-passed, was the home of the Simpsons, whose daughter Margaret married Thomas de Quincey under rather forced circumstances, much to the disapproval of the Wordsworths. Later the cottage was the home of Hartley Coleridge whose neglected sonnets are thought by some to be of the first rank.

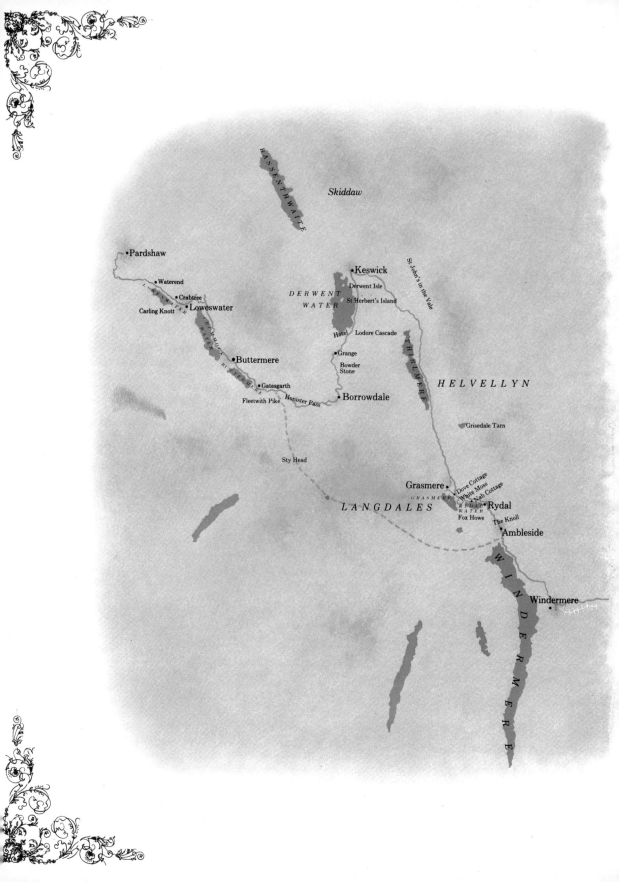

Just beyond the car park on the right a road goes over by White Moss and down past Dove Cottage. This road is to some extent a secret and is unfrequented by central Lakeland standards. It is the way that William and Dorothy would have used. If you take this route you will pass the Wishing Gate, to which Sarah Hutchinson used to climb when she wanted to escape from Coleridge and the Dove Cottage chaos. Unfortunately the view of Grasmere is much obscured by a plantation but it is still possible to get some idea of the balm that she perhaps experienced. Our party went by the turnpike and reported "the Wishing Gate was not in sight".

The modern road from here to Grasmere is the turnpike of 1832. The junction of the 'new' and the old White Moss road provides the best view of the Lion and the Lamb, two rocks at the summit of Helm Crag towards Dunmail Raise. In season it is impossible to park, or to walk on the pavements but Wordsworthian pilgrims will find the church and its churchyard relatively quiet.

Modern Thirlmere has its admirers but its undertones are, alas, of the unscrupulousness involved in the buying-up of farms and cottages before the construction of the reservoir. The dam was opened in 1894. In 1865 Thirlmere's broad river lake, spanned by a bridge, had "the appearance of intensest gloom ... impressing us with the grand and almost awful solemnity of the outer world". Beside the old lake there lay a stone on which the Wordsworths, Coleridge and others, carved their initials. It has now been moved uphill into the forest and although it is perfectly possible to see it there, the nearest place to park is a mile away. To walk along the road at this point is to court death.

Towards the southern end of Derwent Water we pass the Falls of Lodore, which are not really worth stopping for unless there has been heavy rain. Moreover the Falls are not easy to reach. There is a gate by the hotel but nowhere to park; I think the admission charge has remained unchanged for a century. It is easier to park four hundred yards short of the hotel and make one's way by the path through the woods on the left-hand side of the road. Beatrix Potter fans may like to know that it was from about here that Squirrel Nutkin paddled across on his raft of twigs.

It is a pity that the party did not indulge in another tourist pastime — trying the echo. The hotel at Lodore kept a cannon for the purpose: there was an 'economy' version at only 2/6d and a 'super-extra-double-superfine' at 4/-d (equivalent to about £5 and £8 today).

Turner's view of Derwent Water and "the tumbling tide of dread Lodore". Samuel Rogers' poems were very popular in the mid-19th century, and vignettes of this type did much to condition sensibilities.

The Bowder Stone, Borrowdale, by Thomas C. Dibdin (1810-1893). It has been estimated that the stone weighs 1,970 tons, but this illustration follows the usual rather fanciful style of views at this period.

The Bowder Stone, formerly a great attraction, exudes the sorrow of a has-been. There is a track to its left, or eastern, side which may be the old road. It gives one a vivid impression of what Lakeland roads were like in the last century. There are many tracks, now left to walkers, that converge on the Honister Pass. They have served pack

horses, whisky smugglers and the black lead (graphite) mines above Seathwaite. The coach road is almost the same get-out-and-push affair that it was when our party successfully assaulted it. At the top, the same slate quarries have been in production since 1643, although arrangements for getting the slate to the road have since altered. In the 19th century the slates were loaded on to sledges and slithered down the precipitous mountainside. There have been a number of staggering figures quoted: in 1864 Joseph Clarke of Stonethwaite in one day brought down five tons of slate in seventeen separate journeys.

Gatesgarthdale is a desolate, almost lunar, landscape. In high summer the evening sun shines right up the dale and one is encouraged to linger before reaching the rather more obvious charms of Buttermere. It was 5.30 pm by the time our travellers reached the lake, some three hours after leaving Lodore.

The hamlet consists largely of a few hotels, a small church and a legend: the Beauty of Buttermere, whose father was landlord of The Fish Inn, was 'discovered' in 1792 by Joseph Budworth, an early traveller. The resulting publicity attracted an adventurer, one Hadfield. This imposter was actually 'on the run' but he managed to marry The Beauty — only to be later apprehended and eventually hanged for illegally franking letters as a bogus MP. The Beauty herself married again happily and lived her life out round the back of Skiddaw, at Caldbeck.

Although refreshments had been taken *en route*, I suspect that our party would have been in no state to appreciate the beauty of Crummock Water. Nor surprisingly is it

Honister Crag by Thomas Allom. "The descent into Gatesgarth, immediately under Honister Crag, causes one of the sublimest impressions which this country can produce." The crag has been developed as a quarry for the beautiful Honister green slates since the 17th century. This foray did not take place. Marauding Scots avoided the mountains and raided on routes to either side, where defensive pele towers are to be found.

Mill Beck, and Buttermere Chapel, Cumberland by George Pickering (c. 1794-1857). This view has been used by Mary Hodgson. One wonders how wide was the circulation of these engravings. Once the copper had been faced with steel, the number of impressions taken could run into thousands without loss of quality.

mentioned that John Burnyeat, a Quaker who preached all over England, Ireland, Barbados and Maryland, was born at Crabtree, at the south-east end of Loweswater.

It is difficult to try and locate which of the farms was Robert Jackson's. Nor can one say with certainty by which route the party went to Pardshaw Crags on Sunday to try the accoustics and to remember George Fox, who preached there in the open air. It requires an effort of will to imagine the scene. Although the illumination in the journal gives one some ideas the place is overgrown and overgrazed and is not now conducive to reflections on religious intolerance.

The ascent of Carling Knott, or Blake Fell, which our party undertook on Sunday afternoon, is now best made past the Kirk Stile Inn, though the view is not guaranteed. Previously mined for iron-ore, with attendant light railway, the area is now the scene of Forestry Commission activities. Enthusiasts should read Arthur Wainwright's *Guide to the Western Fells.* His forthright views reflect the ongoing 'exchange of views' about reafforestation. The less rigorous should notice "lovely cascade" of woods on the south side of the Water, through which there is a path. Indeed, the Water can be circumnavigated, and the road is not dangerous.

A 6 am start for the return over the same route took them past Crummock Water and Buttermere without a pause. At the top of the Honister Pass a number made off towards Sty Head Pass, with the intention of seeing the Langdales and reuniting at Ambleside. By 20th-century standards, this must have been a considerable forced march by a quite unsuitably equipped party.

Borrowdale and Derwent Water lie in what was once an area of ancient industry. Neolithic axe factories are usually located at higher altitudes and it is thought that the products went down to the sea at Ravenglass for export.

Axes have been found by the Baltic which makes one wonder whether some may have gone by High Street, the Eden Valley settlements and an east coast route.

In the 16th century, Grange-in-Borrowdale was an important copper mining area. German miners first lived on Derwent Isle (for a summer and two winters) to avoid the

St Herbert's Isle, in Derwent Water. Pilgrims came from as far as Lindisfarne to visit the shrine of the Hermit. Turner's vignette, from 'Poems' by Samuel Rogers (1834), is extremely Romantic. No chapel like this has actually existed.

hostility directed at all 'offcomers' then and now. Later they intermarried. Copper and lead have also been mined on the western side of Derwent Water, and at one time the ore from the Greenside mine above Glenridding, by Ullswater, was brought by packhorse over the mountains to be smelted here. At the same time there were a fair number of woodland industries, gunpowder production, and bobbin manufacturing.

Nature heals very quickly and in the late 20th century only the specialist eye can recognize the signs of such industrial activities. Indeed, it is difficult to imagine the shores of Derwent Water unwooded. After the Rising of 1715 the estates of the Earl of Derwentwater were forfeit to the Crown, and given to Greenwich, whose trustees cut down all the timber.

Before leaving Derwent Water I should mention that its islands have their own legends, particularly that of 'Saint Herbert the Lone' and Saint Cuthbert. The two were friends who had prayed together that they might both die on the same day. Herbert was a hermit, and Cuthbert, Prior of Lindisfarne. They did indeed die at the same time in 687, but on opposite sides of the country. It is this story, from Bede, that inspired Turner's illustration to Rogers' *Poems*.

The party spent some hours in Keswick, having their photographs taken and rowing on the lake. The village was even then tourist-orientated, but the pencil factory — the dominant industry after the destruction of the smelters by Parliamentarians (probably in 1648) — still "drives a brisk trade", though they no longer use the black lead from the mines above Borrowdale. The season then was much

shorter than it is today, and the mineralogists who catered for the growing romantic interest in geology were obliged to double as Aeolian harp manufacturers. There are still mineralogists in Keswick, but there are also fast-food outlets, Scottish woollens, climbers' shops and one of the best shoe shops in the country. Now, as then, Keswick is a village in winter and a town in summer, and there are attendant problems.

The Vale of Keswick and Crosthwaite church from Applethwaite by Henry Gastineau. Applethwaite lies under Skiddaw, and this view looks towards the south over Derwent Water. Gastineau, who died in 1876, was closely connected with JMW Turner and others of the English water-colour school.

Castle Rock, Vale of St John, looking South by Thomas Allom.
The two Arthurian knights are an example of Allom's habit of
introducing historical incidents, real or imagined, into his
topographical pictures.

Some of the party then made their way to Greta Hall,
Southey's home for forty years, and now part of a school,
and they then progressed on to see the poet's memorial in
Crosthwaite church. Those fortunate enough to be shown
round the Hall will see the window in which Coleridge fixed
his harp to let the wind play across the strings, and through

which he gazed on the night he wrote *Dejection*, to some the finest Romantic poem in the English language.

Back on the coach road, the party were able to admire the vanishing prospects of Skiddaw and Saddleback (Skiddleback according to Norman Nicholson), looking as if they were clothed in rhinocerous hide. The summit of Skiddaw is the place to celebrate royal weddings and famous victories. On 21st August 1815, Waterloo was celebrated there, and Wordsworth, who kicked the kettle off the fire, "thought to slink off undiscovered". Those expecting a drink of punch were obliged to take it neat with disastrous consequences.

Towards Thirlmere at the junction of St John's in the Vale, the party passed under the Castle Rock of Triermain, a reminder of Sir Walter Scott's *Bridge of Triermain*. Somewhere along this road is the farmhouse in the garden of which, on a cold March night, de Quincey came upon a man moonbathing in an armchair.

To view the Lake District properly, preferably at no more than seven miles per hour, you must travel each road in both directions. The view from Dunmail Raise towards Grasmere is quite different from the view the other way — as our tourists noted. The Raise is a lonely spot, worse in rain, but it is the starting point of the path up to Grisedale tarn and the track down to Patterdale. The pile of stones between the carriageways marks the spot where King Dunmail ("Dunmail the Brave" in Mary Hodgson's poem in the journal) is supposed to have fallen in 945 resisting Edmund of Wessex. In fact he reigned again in Strathclyde and died in Rome.

Dunmail Raise, Cumberland. Grasmere lies in the distance. Dunmail Raise lies on the borders of Cumberland and Westmorland.

Wordsworth and de Quincey used to walk up from Grasmere to meet the wagon bringing the London newspapers. An ear to the ground could detect the vibrations of the wagon's approach at a considerable distance. Since these expeditions usually took place under the stars, the sense of anticipation was considerably heightened.

The party's next stop was Grasmere churchyard, after a number of "pleasant little loiterings" — their gathering of white harebells and tufts of ferns might nowadays lead to a substantial fine! Grasmere churchyard, a retreat from the crowds in summer, is, of course, something of a literary shrine for here are buried William and Dorothy, his daughter and her husband, and little Hartley Coleridge.

On 19 July 1855, Nathaniel Hawthorne passed by Rydal Water remarking, with self-confessed American scorn and some dismay, that it looked like a napkin rather than a sheet of water. He did, however, make the sensible point that these small lakes should best lie still, reflecting the scenery about them. When rippled with a breeze, they can look "dull and sulky, like a child out of humor".

At Ambleside they dined, and were presumably joined by the Langdale expedition. The sun had shone, so they must have had a good day, but by now it was raining, and the farewell views were somewhat marred. Kendal and its castle, however, could be seen from the train. The nature of its stone makes Kendal a rather grey town, and the view would not be enhanced by the weather. Kendal Castle, partly demolished about 1553, was built originally as a defence against Scots depredation, though most of what is left dates from the 13th and 14th century. It was the birthplace of Katherine Parr, the only wife of Henry VIII to survive him in wedlock.

Mary Hodgson's drawing of the Kent estuary towards Lancaster gives a good idea of the view of the Lakeland hills across an arm of Morecambe Bay. This prospect is better seen coming than going, as it is one of the best 'tasters' to

Pen-and-ink drawing by John Harden of Wordsworth's Stamp Office,
Ambleside, in 1834. This is the road for Hawkshead, not travelled by
the party, but no doubt travelled by the Langdale expedition on their return.

whet the appetite. Even better, however, is to cross the Sands at low tide — but not without a guide; quicksands have a malign habit of changing their positions.

Although Lakeland more than holds its own as a magnet for day trippers and weekenders, the towns tend to choke on their urban attractions. Many visitors manage a short 'inside-of-a-day' as they are rushed towards the Trossachs. I am reminded of the gentleman recorded by Joseph Budworth: "Good God! how delightful! — how charming! — I would like to live here forever! Row on, row on, row on, row on!"

There is enough in Lakeland to last a lifetime. In spite of changing tastes, those who seek to rediscover it will find their perceptions enhanced by this mid-Victorian journal. To retrace the journey today takes less than a quarter of the time it took our party but perhaps we derive less from the experience and we certainly record, on our videos and films, images infinitely less evocative of the Spirit of the Lakes than *Excursion to Loweswater*.

Two Essays

read at the

Friends' Institute

Manchester.

12th. month 15th. 1865.

Manchester, 3rd month, 1866.

Dear Friends,

Robert and Rachel Jackson :—

In asking your favourable reception of these Essays, written by two of our number, we are desirous of expressing in a more permanent form than we have yet done, our sense of your great kindness in inviting us to become your guests last summer, and the pleasure the visit afforded to all who were able to accept your large hospitality : whilst we who were not able to be of the party, are equally desirous to unite in this expression of thanks, believing that many pleasant recollections will thus be revived of the large family that invaded your peaceful shores and took possession of your secluded home, with almost everything in the way of food and clothing available therein.

If these rapid but faithful sketches of three delightful days spent with you and in going and returning, should restore to memory some pleasing incidents, as they have done with us, we trust they will not have been written or sent in vain.

With much love

We are,

Your obliged friends,

Jane Atkinson,

Maria Atkinson,

Sarah Maria Brockbank,

Elizabeth Bowles Bryce

Mary Bryce

Charles Collinson

Rachel Maria Corbett

Jonathan Davy

Arthur Jewell Freeman

Mary Matilda Freeman

Lucy Ann Freeman

James Hadfield

John Hodgson

Mary Jane Hodgson

Emily Hodgson

Mary Hodgson

Elizabeth King

Robert Swire Lees

Robert Longdon

Henry Lunt

Lydia Moss Lunt

Martha Godfrey Lunt

Elizabeth Matthews

Catherine Macdougal

Walter Morris

Mary Morris

Jane Morris

Isaac Stevenson Neave

John Henry Neave

Charles Neave

Joseph Boardman Smith

Philip Smith

Joseph Simpson

George Simpson

William Simpson

Hannah Simpson

Joseph Wain

Robert Wilkinson

Samuel Benson Woodhead

Godfrey Woodhead Jun.

Elizabeth Woodhead

Henry Woodhead

Lucy Anne Woodhead.

*John Hargrave

*Thomas Harrison

SKETCHES DURING THREE DAYS AT THE LAKES.

A pleasant thing generally, is a summer excursion, both at the time, and afterwards to look back upon; and a very pleasant one indeed was that undertaken by the Manchester First-day School Teachers towards the close of last Seventh month, into the splendid northern county of "canny auld Cumberland." No part of the country is better suited to an enjoyable summer out than that is, of course providing the weather be all that could be desired; and though in our case it was of a very varied character, as many of us could testify, still we derived a very great amount of interest and enjoyment from our three days' tour. It was not entered upon without a good deal of previous arrangement and forethought, and came about in this wise:-

A friend living at the head of Loweswater had sent us a kind invitation to visit him and his wife at Waterend, and spend a First-day and a couple of nights with them, generously undertaking to provide accommodation for a party of fifty, of course in true picnic fashion. The invitation was joyously received, but the possibility of accepting it was another matter. Many difficulties seemed to rise in the way, and our prospects for some time were anything but clear.

However, thanks to our noble-hearted friends, it was finally pulled through, the various obstacles were smoothed away, the programme of the journey drawn out, the Railway Company was beaten down to the last farthing, and the way satisfactorily opened to get to Loweswater. Forty-four numbered the party;

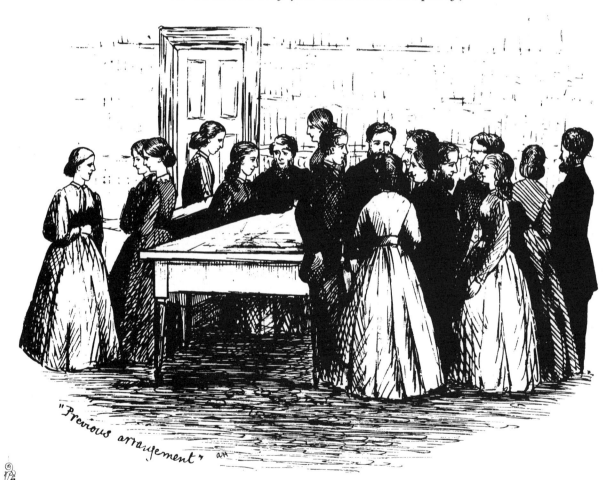

"Previous arrangement" respecting the excursion

seventeen ladies, twenty-seven gentlemen. The time for starting was two o'clock on seventh day morning, with the option of going the night before for any who chose so to do. Twenty-five were of that mind, and the 5.15 train on sixth day evening bore them off to Ambleside. Shall I say how all eyes eagerly scanned the clouds which, alas! looked dark and lowering on all sides, and how, in spite of their threatening aspect, we still clung to the delusive hope that it would no doubt be fine at the end of the journey? Such was not our experience;— as we got further north, the rain came down thick and fast, and we sorrowfully gave up all thoughts of seeing the glorious mountains that night.

Leaving the train at Windermere, we found conveyances waiting to take us on to Ambleside, where we arrived after a long dreary drive, during which the shades of night had closed over us. Of course we saw nothing on the way, except a glimpse now and then of the Lake through the trees which hung in dark, shadowy masses over the road, or the outline of some bold height which rose up black and solemn from out the darkness, and which those who had come that way before,

Felicia Dorothea Hemans
late of Dove's Nest, Windermere

Road to Ambleside, near Dove's Nest

informed us was Loughrigg Fell, or Wansfell Pike,
&c. &c.; and the thought of being so near to them,
with the possibility of climbing to their summits, was
almost too much for the somewhat weary travellers of
one conveyance.

"Snug quarters", Brown's Hotel, Ambleside

Ten o'clock found us in very snug quarters at Brown's Hotel, where it was pleasant to rest, and feel that we had to take no more thought for ourselves, but just do what we were told, — and submit quietly to be very well looked after. I am sure we were all greatly obliged to our valuable friend J.H. for his kind care of us that night, as well as on many occasions afterwards.

Stock Gill Force, under Wansfell, Ambleside

forty-six

During supper-time, we talked of many things, of course; and amongst them of what we should do the next day, and various plans were laid for seeing as much as we could before breakfast, if the morning were favourable. Some quite hoped to ascend Loughrigg Fell;— others proposed a boat on the lake, and a dozen or more arranged to visit Stock-Gill Force, a fine waterfall not far distant. After endless small but ludicrous adventures, which there is neither time nor space to mention, we finally settled for the night.

At six the following morning we were vigorously 'knocked up', and not a little damped at the sight of the rain still falling. All did not turn out then by any means, but others managed to see a good deal, and get to the Waterfall as well, though it had to be done under umbrellas, and over very moist ground. We wended our way up-hill through a copsewood, and by and bye came face to face with the fall, which was a fine sight, though owing to the long, dry season, it had not by any means its full quantity of water. The trees and masses of foliage that hung over it looked very beautiful, the rain giving them such a fresh greenness, which added to the loveliness of their leafy summer glory. We gathered lots of moss which grew luxuriantly on the rocks and stones at our feet, and which, I am sorry to say, died afterwards in the bottom of the waggonettes.

Mill at Ambleside

Mill on the Stock Gill

Returning to breakfast, we were there joined by the remainder of the party, who had just arrived from Manchester by the early train, looking rather jaded, perhaps, but still in very good trim for the day's work; and not much time elapsed before we were all on the way to Rydal, our cortège consisting of five wagonettes, each with two horses, and a one-horse phaëton. Of course the umbrellas were all up, and I have no doubt but that we were looked upon as a melancholy sight by the country-folk as we passed along;— certainly we felt nothing of it ourselves, though a certain amount of regret existed over the weather, and we began to fear that the feast of beauty for which our eyes had prepared was likely to prove of a very limited character.

Still the little we could see was very grand, and now and then the clouds rose and revealed some magnificent outlines and bare black mountain sides, with perhaps here and there a bright patch of green. Fell rose above fell in wild

William Wordsworth

and rugged sublimity, and stretched far away beyond where our eyes could reach; and we concluded that the face of Nature was indeed surpassingly beautiful, and that we could scarcely wish it otherwise.

You will readily imagine that our enjoyment was everything that could be desired; omitting, perhaps, the drips from the umbrellas.

Passing Glen Rothay, the residence of William Ball, one of our conductors sent in a message to the effect that "a friend or two from Manchester would be glad to see him"; but, unfortunately, he was not at home, so we pursued our way.

We had now a fine view of the towering height of Knab Scar, with Rydal Mount, Wordsworth's dwelling, a lovely spot hidden in trees, roses, and ivy; and away to the right stretched the Loughrigg Fells, while beyond Knab Scar were the heights of Fairfield.

Rounding a bend in the road, we get a view of Grasmere, and Grasmere Church, and of course we begin to talk about Wordsworth's grave in the quiet churchyard, and his cottage; and we eagerly look round for the latter, till our obliging driver points it out to us. The Wishing-Gate was not in sight.

Grasmere is a beautiful lake, with Helm Crag, or the Lion and Lamb, rising at the head; a noble

Rydal Mount, home of the late William Wordsworth

View towards Fairfield from Fox How, once the residence
of Thomas Arnold

Approach to Rydal, Westmorland

Grasmere, Westmorland

eminence which we felt sorry we could not see to the best advantage, though the rain had ceased now, and the sun actually shone out on the mountains for a little while, clothing them with all manner of beautiful colours.

fifty-four

Head of Derwentwater and Lodore from the Lake, in 1860

The roads being hilly, the gentlemen varied
the journey by now and then getting out to walk,
scrambling after ferns and harebells, or scooping
in the lake for shells, and so on, till we reached
Thirlmere, a long narrow lake with a small lone
island at one end, black solemn-looking water, and
equally black mountains, amongst which the Eagle
Crag reared its frowning precipices to the wild heavy
clouds above, giving to the scene the appearance of
intensest gloom, and again impressing us with the
grand and almost awful solemnity of the outer world.

"Life is a changing scene"; and so it proved with us that day, for the little town of Keswick was in the full enjoyment of a brilliant summer noon-tide when we drove through the market-place, causing the quiet townsfolk to look up at the long procession as it passed on its way to Lodore.

Here we spent three hours; dining in a large unromantic wooden house in the garden of the Hotel, and afterwards visiting the waterfall and rowing on the Lake: but the particulars of the rest of the journey we quote from the diary of one of the party:-

"On the lake" near Lodore

2.30 p.m. Hotel at Lodore

"We are all once more assembled, after making raids in various directions; some to the very top of the Waterfall, where the ladies sang songs among the rocks, and the echoes woke up to join in the applause.

There have been two attempts at rowing, neither very successful, as a thick mist came suddenly down, and covered up everything, damping us generally.

The order to start has gone forth. We pack up, open the umbrellas, and take our seats, the rain pouring.

Prospects — not the most cheering.

Rosthwaite in Borrowdale

"The road is so steep and difficult"

3.25 p.m. Entering Borrowdale.

A fearful storm raging. Nothing but clouds, and such awful crags, down which newly-formed mountain torrents are dashing, which rush over the rocks and stones in our path, and look like rapids.

We are getting dreadfully wet, and think that we had better not have come!

The road is so steep and difficult, that our drivers say we must get out, and walk. This is a terrific announcement, but there is nothing else for us.

We must try to keep our feet as well as we can. Certainly no easy matter; the wind against us, the rain pelting down unmercifully, umbrellas next to no use, continually going inside out.

We are wet through, complete sops.

Some one wonders whether our friends are thinking of us at home, and if they could see their forlorn relations in Borrowdale, whether they would most pity or laugh at them!

Alas for certain white hats!

3.40 p.m. Some of the gentlemen, feeling for the pitiable condition of the ladies, petitioned the driver of one of the conveyances to allow them to get in,

Scale Force, Buttermere

which they gladly do; but the bumping over the great stones was so fearful, they were in momentary dread of being pitched over into the little river below, so again turn out to try the walking.

We have just caught a little glimpse of Honister Crag through a rift in a cloud.

4.25   We are now over the worst, and feel quite inclined to "rest and be thankful".

We all take our seats in the wagonettes, and quietly drip into the bottom.

Rain still pouring.

4.45   We arrive at Gatesgarth, and stop a little while for refreshments;— then on again, through a magnificent country, but oh, so wild!

Intense amusement prevails over our crushed and dilapidated appearance, and we all laugh at one another without any unpleasant consequences ensuing.

5.30   Passing Buttermere.

A small portion of Great Gable in sight.

Buttermere

A kind friend in our conveyance entertains the company with the tragic story of 'Mary of Buttermere,' and random guesses are made about her cottage.

Intensely black mountains rise from the Lake, whose water is equally black with the reflection from them.

6.10 Rounding a bold promontory, we now get a splendid view of Crummock Water, with Melbreak in front, looking so grand, and Whiteless Pike, Grassmoor, and Whiteside on the right. We get quite enthusiastic over them, in spite of our depressing condition.

Loweswater is not far off, and our spirits are rising in consequence.

7.10 A cry has been raised in front that Waterend is in sight. Joyful sound!

We straighten up instantly, and try to make as respectable an appearance as our circumstances will allow.

No rain now; and in the sky before us is a long streak of bright golden light.

7.30 We drive up to R. Jackson's; kind friends come out to meet us, and overwhelm us with sympathy.

The sky clear, and the hills are bathed in sunshine.

Our sorrows are all over now!'

It was delightful to reach the end of our journey; but oh! the commotion we brought to that peaceful dwelling!

Roadside by Crummock Water, "A bold promontory"

"A bold promontory"

Mill Beck and Buttermere Chapel

View of Crummock Water and Buttermere from Lowfell, above Loweswater

Certainly never before had forty-four such pitiable objects crossed that threshold! and possibly never may again.

One after another of the wagonettes was emptied rapidly of the wet and miry occupants, and a warm and hearty greeting at the door bade each one welcome.

Then indeed was there a rushing to and fro to provide relief and comfort for all that distressed multitude; and kind and willing hands, which we can never sufficiently thank, all united to improve as far as lay in their power our sorrowful condition.

But how shall we speak of that wonderful and inexhaustible wardrobe, from which garments were forthcoming without number, and of many sorts and sizes to satisfy all demands:— which rose in a towering eminence before the delighted gaze of the surrounding suppliants, who came flocking one after the other to carry off from the fast diminishing pile, what best suited their various requirements; and if the fit was not the most exact, what did it matter? It only added to the general merriment, and peals of merriest laughter rang round. For who would not have laughed on such an occasion? Truly it baffles description; and not very often, we may safely say, shall we look upon its like again!

Very pleasant was the assembling round the well-spread supper tables, to enjoy what was so bountifully provided for us. How we talked over all we had gone through, and laughed again at the ludicrous costumes which figured here and there amongst us, and finally we concluded that we never possibly could spend such another day as the one that was then terminating so satisfactorily. And when supper was over, and all had done justice to the liberal and elegant fare, don't we rejoice to remember, that the last touch was added to the picture when the master, after a solemn pause, read the beautiful words which long ago fell from the lips of his Master and ours:-

"Let not your heart be troubled; ye believe in God, believe also in me."

Rest being very acceptable to the weary travellers, they soon retired for the night, and silence reigned over the large household, while the moon shone peacefully down upon the mountains, and left a long silvery sheen on the lake.

First-day morning rose beautiful, cheering us all, and promising a lovely day. Of course we went to meeting, and a pleasant drive it was to Pardshaw over an undulating country road, and in the fresh, bright morning air.

Supper at Waterend on 29 July 1865

The primitive simplicity of the little meeting-house was something quite refreshing, as well as the warm greeting from many of its worthy attenders, whose numbers were considerably increased by the presence of such an "unnumbered multitude."

Our assembling there was an event to be remembered, and long will be, I am sure, by all of us, with the glowing words of a minister from America, who met us there, and with powerful inspiration addressed

"the children of our people, come up to see the works of God."

It was a nice solemn time, and among the pleasant and profitable experiences of that eventful excursion, not the first to be forgotten will be the little meeting at Pardshaw.

Afterwards we were all conducted to the wonderful Pardshaw Crags, and stood before the stone pulpit from which our illustrious ancestor proclaimed the Gospel to the thousands in the meadow below.

The views around were splendid, and having seen everything, we returned to Waterend to dinner; which being over, the company laid themselves out in picturesque groups on the grass around our hostess, and beguiled the time with hymns and recitations.

"The moon shines peacefully down upon the mountains"

"Picturesque groups on the grass"
After dinner on First Day the 30th

While some of Whittier's beautiful lines fix their attention, we can take a few notes of the sublime region before us.

Just below is the Lake, so clear and blue, and mirror-like; now reflecting the little, light clouds which glide gently over its smooth surface, and again ruffled into tiny eddies by the dipping swallows, but all the time looking so perfectly at rest.

And then the mountains, which rise in strength and might around it, and are piled up one above another, till far away in the dim distance their shapes mingle with the clouds and are lost to us. But my feeble pen cannot describe them; and to one who has seen them they need no description.

Our enthusiasm culminated when we had fairly ascended to the summit of Carling Knot (Blake Fell), one of the highest points on the opposite side of the lake. The climbing was tremendous, but we were well repaid when we reached the top, and saw the magnificent view there is from it.

I can give no idea of it, so will simply say that looking to the West, there was the Isle of Man, the Solway Frith, and the Scotch hills, laid out like a beautiful panorama; and behind, Scawfell Pike, Red Pike, Helvellyn, and an endless assemblage of mountain tops, all covered with a rich sunset haze.

Loweswater from Waterend

We stood long to look at them, while our feet sank
in the soft moss, and the little black-faced sheep
bleated near us, the only sound that broke the
intense stillness.

"The climbing was tremendous"
The ascent of Carling Knot

"Obliged to descend rapidly"

After enjoying ourselves in this somewhat romantic fashion, we were obliged to tear ourselves away, and descend rapidly to our comfortable quarters for the night, with the one agonizing thought that we must leave them early the following morning....Here let me pause, to add my small meed of gratitude to that which will be felt by the company generally, for the kindness and attention of our hospitable entertainers; and I am sure that their exceeding great care over us, had not a little to do with our enjoyment while with them.

At 4 a.m on second day, all was astir at Waterend; and in two hours, the long cavalcade, after three hearty cheers for our hosts, turned face homewards; no wonder that they did so reluctantly. We had a glorious day, and saw everything under a different aspect from our seventh day's experience.

Again we pass over Borrowdale; but no umbrellas to be seen now, no disasters or humiliations this time; on, past the Bowder Stone, past Lodore, and along Derwentwater, to Keswick, with the many-topped Skiddaw lifting its gigantic bulk beyond the foot of the lake. I have no words left to speak of its wondrous beauty; but it seems to me that to row on Derwentwater as we did then, or climb the Castle Hill and see Skiddaw as it looked that day with the sun beaming down upon it, would be one of the most delightful of all enjoyments.

Castle Crag in Borrowdale

Castle Crag near the entrance to Borrowdale

*Among our adventures at Keswick, perhaps
we might mention one of a peculiarly interesting
character, which was, that a certain party of 'Ten'
who gallantly stood by one another through all the
perils and pleasures of that eventful journey, wishing
to shew their due appreciation of the place and its
inhabitants, as well as to encourage the rising genius
of a youthful artist, paid him a visit, and sat for their
photographs, which were quickly taken in an artistic
group, and have since occupied a place in many of
our albums, affording us each time we look upon*

Bridge over the Greta, Keswick

seventy-seven

Skiddaw, from the village of Applethwaite, Cumberland

them some new source of delight and amusement,
and bringing back with vivid freshness those
wonderful Lake experiences.

Departing from Keswick, our course lay for miles
along the undulating coach-road; and truly delightful
was this part of our return journeying; the scenery
was so magnificent, and the day so lovely, and there
seemed nothing to interrupt our enjoyment.

Certainly it was sad to have to bid adieu to
Skiddaw, and very regretfully did we take our last
look at her towering, 'sun-crowned' summit, before
a bend in the road hid her finally from our sight.
Not to be forgotten, however, was her peerless
majesty, rather to return with an added glory
to many of our after musings.

As we went along, we now and then took time for
pleasant little loiterings, and got down from our seats
to gather sweet white harebells, and luxuriant tufts of
fern that grew abundantly beside the way, some of
which happily still survive, though so far removed
from their native mountain air.

So the hours sped:— we had passed under the
"brow of the mighty Helvellyn", and under many
other noble but to some of us nameless summits,
when Grasmere once more spread her enchanting
surface before us, and exquisite indeed was the blue

Derwentwater, from the Castle Hill, or Castlet,
near Keswick

"The mighty Helvellyn" with Thirlmere

"The Poets' Corner" in Grasmere Churchyard.

*of her waters, and the warm, sunny slopes of her
mountains. But perhaps our attention was this time
more closely directed to the Poets' Corner of the
churchyard, whither we repaired to linger awhile
beside Wordsworth's grave, and that of his gentle
daughter Dora, and poor Hartley Coleridge.
Delightfully calm and peaceful is the last earthly
resting-place of these whose memories we so
faithfully cherish. We thought so, as we stood there,
and, it maybe, contrasted it too with the scene of
storm and tumult that life had been to at least one of
those quiet sleepers, for in his case*

> *'Earth has given her calm
> To whom she gave her anguish.'*

eighty-two

Knab Cottage, Rydal Water
once home of Hartley Coleridge

*Perhaps such thoughts somewhat subdued
our mirth during the remainder of our drive to
Ambleside. There arriving, it was trying to find
that ominous clouds were gathering, and heavy
raindrops beginning to fall, as we once more entered
the spacious Hotel to sit down to dinner, over which
meal no time was to be lost, as the hour of six was
to witness our departure by train from Windermere,
and a considerable space was required to get to
the station.*

Head of Stock Gill, Ambleside

We grieved indeed to think that after all our glowing anticipations of a fine evening, rain and storm were to be our portion. No glorious lines of fading sunlight on the mountains were to gladden our eyes on departing, much as we had longed to see them, and the gloom that was spread over the lake was perhaps communicated to our spirits to some extent, for very many of us would fain have

tarried longer in that region of so much beauty and delight, and nothing was so solacing, on being borne away so rapidly, as plunging into some of our past experiences, and enjoying, in delicious mental picturings, that which was no more visible to our outward sight.

Not, we trust without deep feelings of joy and gratitude did we enter our beloved Manchester that night, and its tall chimneys had long been shrouded in darkness and mist ere our party reached their homes.

Of course we all felt we had had a most splendid out, and such had truly been the case.

Nor are its pleasures at all likely soon to be forgotten; far into our lives will go the remembrance of that delightful tour, taking with it heart-felt thanks and gratitude to all those who so admirably cared for us, the kind friends who pioneered our way, and the dear and honoured dwellers at Waterend, to whom we shall ever owe all the intense enjoyments of that thoroughly halcyon time, our three days at the Lakes.

written by L M Lunt

LML
Manchester
12th Month 1865

THREE DAYS IN LAKELAND

Dear friends who have roved in the shadow
beloved
Of England's north-westerly heights,
Can we ever forget what comes back to us yet
In varied and exquisite lights?
Or the kindness and thoughtful exertions of
those
Who asked us our Manchester labours to close,
For a time, to admire the splendid repose
Of their country's ineffable sights?
Yet we who went forth to that beautiful North
In a party of forty and four,
Not unwilling may be a description to see

"our Manchester Labours to Close."

(Joseph A. Forster)

eighty-seven

Of the days that so quickly were o'er,
Days like unto which it is possible we
Had never encountered before.

On the twenty-eighth day of the seventh month last,
The first of our company started;
Sweet Ambleside gave them a shelter that eve;
While the rest (though it really is hard to believe),
At two the next morning departed.
But we, whether later or earlier, met
With magnificent mountains around us,
And the hour of eight, or a little more late,
In company breakfasting found us.
We had looked upon Windermere, sovereign Lake,
With her wide-spreading northerly shore;
We had passed through the woods on her easterly side

Approach to Ambleside

Windermere
from Low Wood

To the shadows of Wansfell and more;
And some of us went to the perilous rent,
Where Stockgill's white waters were nearly
                    outspent,
    For dry were the streams on the moor.

When breakfast was over, with little delay
Six carriages came to conduct us away,
For long was the journey before us that day.

Undamped in our spirits by ominous rain,
    From Ambleside swiftly we drove;
Thence passing to Rydal through scenery grand,
    For which we redoubled our love
As we thought of the good and the great of the
                    land,

Rydal Water
Under Loughrigg
From a photograph by J. B. Forster

Who once in that valley did rove.
Of Wordsworth, who over each beautiful scene
      Has woven the wreath of a song ;
And the honoured of Rugby, who loved his
          retreat

      The woodlands of Loughrigg among,
Whence he looked upon Fairfield's majestical
          form,
Or the Red Screes of Kirkstone attracting the storm,
Or the lovely hill-side where the Flemings reside
      By waterfalls dashing and strong.

We gazed up in awe to the top of Knab Scar,
On whose slope was the home of the Westmorland
          star
      Above Rydal's fair hamlet and small ;

"Sweet waters"
Grasmere from Loughrigg

ninety-four

And the clear stream of Rothay at foot of
the fell,
Near the house of a friend who is known to us
well,
For who could forget him at all,
Or what he composed on his favourite steep,
An epitaph meant for the public to read
On a tablet enshrined in the wall?
Perusing it made us but little dejected;
For the Westmorland lakelets ere then we detected,
With fairest of isles in the waters reflected.

Still onward, and northward, we joyously sped,
Till Grasmere before was enchantingly spread.
And where can exist, under sunshine or mist,
A more loveable spot in the realm?

Dr Arnold
"The honoured of Rugby"

Fox How
Loughrigg Fell
Westmorland

Sweet waters that circle a fragment of green,
From Red Bank and Silver How shading the
scene,
To the "Lion and Lamb" that are lying serene
'Mid the crags on the summit of Helm.

Up the long, long ascent to the top of the Raise,
We went, looking back o'er the Lake;
Till her place to another our Westmorland gave,
By the great pile of stones o'er the desolate grave
Of the last king of Cumberland, Dunmail the
brave,
A Briton most eager to break
Through Saxon oppression; but failing to save
His country, fell here for her sake.

Dunmail Raise

On the scene of this ancient and perilous fight,
"The mighty 'Helvellyn' looked down from the
right;
While Thirlmere's broad river-lake, spanned by
a bridge,
Lay low at the foot of the giant-like ridge
With a surface that gloomily shone.
Then the tiny white chapel of Wythburn we
passed,
And Saddleback rose with his crevices vast,
As by cataracts made that are gone;
But these and great Skiddaw were partly
o'ercast;
Yet we grieved when it came to our looking
the last
Up the rock-skirted Vale of St. John.

The Vale of St John, & Saddleback

one hundred

The rain had not fallen for many a mile,

When Keswick's fair valley below us did smile

As a vision of beauty and light:

We looked from the road over Castlerigg high,

To where broad-spreading Bassenthwaite peaceful

doth lie,

And Derwent's clear depths, that were nearer

the eye,

And deliciously welcome to sight.

We stayed not in Keswick, but went by the shore,

And Barrow Cascade, to the Inn at Lodore.

In the pretty green garden that gladdens the place,

Is a summer-house, spacious and round;

And there, at this point of our sight-seeing race,

An important diversion we found,

"We looked from the road over Castlerigg high"

one hundred and two

In the shape of a dinner provided with grace

By a kindhearted friend who had pondered our

case.

The pleasant meal over, we wandered about;

There were some who to row on the water went out;

And most of us rose up the cataract rocks,

With many backslidings and wonderful shocks,

Where the Fall is accustomed to roar;

We were sorry so little of water to find

That Southey's description gave grief to the mind,

As we climbed up the steeps of Lodore.

The Fall was nigh empty — the heavens were not;

And descending of rain for a time was our lot

As we drove on our journey away

"we climbed up the steeps of Lodore"

But magnificent Borrowdale lost not her
                    pride ;
Most beautiful she when her mountains can
                    hide
Under mist as a veil, and be dimly espied
        With distancing outlines of grey.

Glaramara's rough peaks, with Great Gable, Great
                    End,
And many bold outworks that rise to defend
        The fortress of mighty Scawfell,
Gaze proudly adown on this valley so grand,
On hamlets and homesteads that peacefully
                    stand
        By streams in the depth of the dell:
From Seatollar we clambered, with scarcely a pause,

"magnificent Borrowdale"

one hundred and six

Up the steep rugged pathway of Borrowdale Haws,
'Twas truly a clamber of wonderful sort,
For the drizzle of mist scarcely troubled our
      sport,
Though of thorough protection we really were
      short,
    And 'twas wonder we bore it so well.

But the bold front of Honister, lofty and steep,
Where high overhead the cool vapours did creep
    Stood out in his grandeur at length;
Below him we drove on a perilous way
To where down in the valley dark Buttermere lay
And where Crummock's deep waters acknowledged
      the sway
    Of Grassmoor's immovable strength.

If smaller than others, in stateliness more,
Dear lakes of the steep side and green wooded
shore!

'Twas by Crummock the misty and mountainous
rain
No longer came drenching our band;
The blue sky broke out in the heavens again,
As we rapidly drove through a bowery lane
To Loweswater's beautiful strand.
And just as from under a vaporous fold
Shone the glories of evening in orange and gold,
To a sweet smiling homestead our wagonettes rolled,
And speedily came to a stand.

There the friends who had asked us their guests to become

Honister Crag
looking N.W.

one hundred and nine

Crummock Water - Cumberland

Buttermere

one hundred and eleven

Gave us warm and delightful reception;
But oh, of our state as we entered their home,
In watered apparel bespattered with loam,
  'Tis hard to give any conception.

Yet kind hands most willingly, busily sought
  To reform our astonishing plight;
A marvellous number of garments were
              brought
To set all the damp and the coldness at nought,
And merriment rose in relation to those
Who entered perceptibly altered in clothes
  'Mid the jubilant circle that night.
And who that was by can the pleasure forget
As round the long bountiful tables we met,
A Cumberland supper to welcome and get?

And the stillness that came over all at the close,
When the head of the house in solemnity rose,
And read from the Book ere we went to
repose ?

"Where rested so many ?" a querist may say,
"After all the fatigues of this wonderful day ?"
There were some in the house were appointed
to stay,
And more on sweet heather the night slept away
In a spacious apartment suggestive of hay.
But whereoer we were when the starlight was
beaming,
Our couch was delightful, and pleasant our
dreaming.

Cockermouth

How bright was the sunlight that came through
the trees

Next morning in midst of our greeting!
And gilded thereby, through a westerly breeze,
We went o'er the moorlands to meeting.
To the village of Pardshow, four miles from
our lake,
And the same from the Cockermouth
steeple;

one hundred and fourteen

To a meeting-house nearly as old as the day
When first we were known as a people.
Substantial the structure, nor wanting in space
For a goodly assembly beside us;
Perchance the white walls on a number so great
Had seldom looked down since the early estate
When attenders were never denied us.
As meeting broke up, it was mostly adjourned
To the Crags from which wonderful eloquence
burned,
And the hearts of assemblies were mightily
turned

To attend to the Spirit within,
By an eminent preacher, who many an hour
Spoke there his great message in heavenly power
A flock for his Master to win.

A remarkable crag of a pulpit-like form
Was the place whence he poured in persuasiveness
warm
His entreaties for banishing sin.

We stood in the pastures at foot of the Rocks,
Being wishful awhile to remain

one hundred and sixteen

Where once were the multitudes hearing
George Fox
By thousands all over the plain.
We listened to some of our number who spake
In varying measure and strain
To know if their voices could certainly make
An audible speech that we could not mistake.
The experiment answered to edification;
For plainly we heard even quiet oration,
Because of the region's peculiar formation.

Returning o'er moors to the Loweswater shore,
We strolled in the garden when dinner was o'er,
Or sat on the sunny green slopes;
The day was most lovely, exceeding by far
In splendour, our liveliest hopes.

"The multitudes hearing George Fox"

So we wandered away to the beautiful woods
    That hang on the west of the mere,
Where a lofty cascade in the depth of the shade
    Is formed by a rivulet clear.
We climbed up the steeps at the side of the fall
    With courage o'ermastering fear.

On emerging at last from the uppermost woods,
    It neither seemed needful nor well
To neglect to proceed with invincible speed
    Till arrived on the top of the Fell.
One after another, on coveted ground
With serious exertion at length we were found
    Observing with eager delight
The prospect below us, above, and around,
    Unusually clear to the sight.

"away to the beautiful woods"

Our station was high, and displayed for the eye
  A truly magnificent feast;
Huge masses of mountains were piercing the sky
  Away to the south and the east,
O'ertopped by the Pikes, that a monarch supply
  To the rest, whether highest or least.

All broad in the West was the exquisite hue
  For hundreds of miles, of the Sea;
Where the grand heights of Mona rose up from
                    the blue,
And over the Solway were clearly in view
The south bays of Scotland, all mountainous too,
  And deeply delighted were we.

The plains of the Shire wherein we did stand

From Carling Knob, to "Where the grand heights of Mona rose up from the blue"

one hundred and twenty-two

Sloped peacefully down to the westerly strand
  And seaports whence smoke did arise:
Indeed, from this mountain (a branch of Blake
      Fell),
'Twas easy the course of the county to tell,
  As far to the northward it lies.
Great Cumberland, scattered thy people may be;
But those who have taken their nurture from thee
  Not seldom are noble and wise.

The sun was inclined his departure to take,
As we swiftly descended once more to the Lake,
  And talked of our deeds over tea;
We followed his light, that our strength might
      revive;
For breakfast next morning precisely at five,

one hundred and twenty-four

And departing at six, were to be.

Being true to our orders, we rose up at four;
All early preparing was rapidly o'er,
And once more the vehicles stood at the door.
Ah, painful the parting that verged upon tears,
While many gave hearty and powerful cheers
    To our hosts as we quitted their home;
Away we were bound, on that day to be found
    In the city from whence we had come.

The Loweswater woods were afar from our sight,
And Crummock and Buttermere's surfaces bright,
As again we were under that monarch of might,
    Steep Honister, sombre and grey;
Our company came to a stand, to behold

Quarryman's Sled

Sled Roads on Honister

A venturesome man, who a wheelbarrow rolled
Down the face of the shale from a slate-bearing
hold
Some hundreds of feet from our way.

On reaching the apex of Honister Pass,
We lost of our number a few;
They went to encounter the Gable's great mass,
And the grandeur of Langdale to view.
We wished them delight as they went from our
sight,
By cheering abundant and true.

one hundred and twenty-six

In Borrowdale's region so bold and sublime,
With pleasure we yielded a fragment of time,
And up to the Bowder Stone managed to climb.

Crosthwaite Church
Keswick

No little sensation our equipage made
While two happy hours in Keswick we staid,
And proceeded its beautiful haunts to invade.

"No little sensation our equipage made"

How lovely is all that encounters the eye
     As we stand upon hills by the Lake;
From Scafell and Skiddaw, to Causey and Bells,
     And the woodlands where cataracts break,
And the purest of waters are stealing around
     The verdure of many an isle,
From one where a Marshall his dwelling has
         found,
To a larger, the Ratcliffe's more wilderness ground,
     Containing a ruinous pile, —
And the centremost patch of St. Herbert the
         lone,

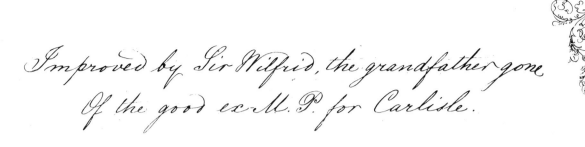

Improved by Sir Wilfrid, the grandfather gone
Of the good ex-M. P. for Carlisle.

Some viewed the fair scene as they rowed o'er
the wave

Among those delectable islands;
And grand was the prospect the clear waters gave
Of the changeable tints of the highlands.
Some passed the long street of the little town
through,

The home of the talented Southey to view;
And Crosthwaite's old church, where an effigy
true

Of the poet in marble is seen;
Enchanting the meadows where wandered the bard,
By Greta's cool waters of clearness unmarred,

Robert Southey.
late of Greta Hall Keswick

"Greta Hall Keswick"

one hundred and thirty

On pathways o'ershadowed with green.

There were others among us, well known as
"the Ten,"
O'erflowing with spirit and glee,
Who at once on arriving, went over the town
A resident artist to see,
Who speedily took them in photograph down,
So that they, ere the time of our staying was
flown,
Were perceived on the water to be.

We parted from Keswick, and southward went
back,
Along the old coach-road's familiar track,
With its exquisite scenery lined;

one hundred and thirty-one

Grasmere Church

one hundred and thirty-two

And this we admired, though many were tired,
And some were perversely inclined
To joke upon others, appearing from far
As a desolate group of our friends in a car
Much given to staying behind.

By the churchyard of Grasmere we eagerly drove,
To visit the graves that we cannot but love,
Where Wordsworth and kinsmen lie low;
With poor Hartley Coleridge, resting beside,
The gifted, the brilliant, who grievously died,
And how, it is painful to know.

Through the great amphitheatred valley at last,
Into Ambleside shelter our company passed,
Where raindrops were falling alarmingly fast

"in our way to the station that day"

one hundred and thirty-four

As vanished our dinner and tea;
Yet we strove on the way to the station that
day,
The queen of the waters to see.
And oh, amid mountains encompassed with
storms,
Rose bright over Langdale the beautiful forms
Of its Pikes, from obscurity free.
To see those grand summits the firmament
cleaving,
Was truly a vision of comfort on leaving.

At six in the evening we sat in the train;
Soon passing the Castle of Kendal again,
And joining the line from Carlisle:
Then farther to southward beamed out on our sight

Lancaster

one hundred and thirty-six

The currents of Morecambe so peacefully bright,
  O'erlooked by the Lancaster pile:—
But great Ingleborough, fair Lonsdale's
          delight,
    Was hidden in vapours the while.
That night about ten, we were settled
          again
    Where the homes of our Manchester
          smile.

That musings were ours at end of the days!
How we thanked the good guides who had cared
          for our ways!
How we gave their exertions unlimited praise.

Of natural glory how vain is a story;

Elleray Windermere

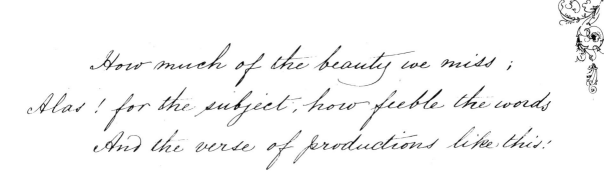

How much of the beauty we miss ;
Alas ! for the subject ; how feeble the words
And the verse of productions like this :

The wood-skirted mountain, – the desolate
steep, –
The silvery mere, and the cataract's leap ;
The coast of the West in its exquisite
sweep,
We left in reluctance behind ;
And though now the rich beauty to many
may seem
To have passed from our sight as a marvellous
dream,
'T is deep in the records of mind :
While thoughts of the goodness bestowed on our band

At that lovely abode in the midst of the land,
By friends of kind spirit and liberal hand,
    Are there even deeper enshrined.
Thanks, thanks for that goodness, we
                gratefully say ;
Can we ever our debts in dear Cumberland pay?

Manchester,
    11th mo. 1865.

Morecambe Bay (Kent Estuary) from near Milnthorpe

Commentary on the illustrations
by Christopher Newsom

Felicia Hemans, one of the few people who stood up to Wordsworth, was a poetess who wrote, amongst other things, 'The Boy Stood on the Burning Deck'. She spent a short time in the district, at Doves Nest near the Low Wood Hotel, before returning to Wales.

The engraving from which this has been redrawn is reproduced on page twenty-four of the Introduction. I have no doubt that this is the case with others. The portrait of Coleridge is, for example, a copy of the American Washington Allman's, done at Bristol in 1814.

This scene is drawn from somewhere near the Wishing Gate. See Introduction page nineteen

This is the view from the telephone box.

Hause Point. A considerable amount of rock-blasting was undertaken in the 19th century to open up roads in the Lake District. The old road climbed steeply to the right and descended the other side.

Thirlmere was metamorphosed between 1877 and 1894. At the time the party went by, Manchester's City Fathers were just beginning to appreciate the scale of their problem; the demand for water had trebled in a very short time.

This view of Grasmere, from Loughrigg, fails to bring out the Lion and the Lamb. Dunmail Raise is on the right.

Fox How, on that rather gloomy road on the west side of the River Rothay, was the holiday home of Dr Arnold of Rugby, one of the most notable headmasters of the 19th century.

The Langdale Pikes are distant on the right. In the foreground is the Low Wood Hotel. The spiral A591 road runs between the Lake and the Hotel, connecting Bowness-on-Windermere with Ambleside and Keswick. It is, in season, a motorist's nightmare.

This view from Dunmail Raise used a certain amount of licence. The Raise beck by no means leaves the summit with the vigour portrayed. From its position in the journal one might have expected a view of Thirlmere, but it must be Grasmere in the distance.

The Castle Rock of Triermain, mentioned in the Introduction, is on the extreme right. In Sir Walter Scott's poem 'The Bridal of Triermain', King Arthur dallied in a castle which 'Romantically metamorphoses into a rock' according to the dictates of the narrative.

The Falls of Lodore, in a wet season, are rather more impressive than this. In a dry season it is not unknown for searchers-in-vain to be told that they are sitting on them!

Cockermouth Castle successfully resisted its last seige by the Royalists during the Civil War; its owners allowed most of it to fall into disrepair. Cockermouth was the birthplace of William Wordsworth and has many other literary associations. Fletcher Christian of 'Mutiny on the Bounty' fame was educated here.

The lake on the right is Bassenthwaite Lake. Keswick is the middle distance centre. The mountains in the background must include Grisedale Pike and Lord's Seat. Between them, concealed, lies the Whinlatter Pass. The view from the A66 approaching Keswick is possibly more rewarding.

These are Pardshaw Crags; they do not look like this today. It is recorded that in 1857 when Neale Dow, the American temperance reformer, addressed a meeting here the amount of beer consumed broke all records.

one hundred and forty-three

The Isle of Man is rather more distant that this view suggests. It is, in fact, forty-five miles away. Nevertheless, on a clear day the island can be seen and the fact that it was a Norse staging-post between Ireland and Cumbria is appreciated.

Crosthwaite Church, the parish church of Keswick, is one of the most interesting in the area. It was founded by Saint Kentigern in the 6th century, rebuilt in the 12th and last restored by Sir Giles Gilbert Scott in 1844. The church contains many interesting monuments, among which can be noted that to Sir John Radcliffe who 'probably' led the Keswick men at Flodden Field.

Elleray, the home of Professor Wilson (Christopher North) was demolished in 1869. Wilson left, taking up a chair at Edinburgh in 1820, after his fortune was lost by an uncle managing his estate. Essentially an all-round sportsman, his appointment has been described as one of the most scandalous in British academic history.

This drawing of Honister Crag and Fleetwith Pike (centre) was done from Gatesgarth, where the party stopped for refreshments on the outward journey. The modern quarries are more or less directly behind the Pike, as is the path the Langdale expedition took from the top of the Pass.

This part of Morecambe Bay used to be navigable by quite large vessels. Milnthorpe was Westmorland's only port but the steady silting-up of the bay has denied large vessels even the quay at Arnside, from which boats once left for Liverpool.

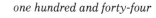